The...

Written by Shane Nagle
Illustrated by Shane Nagle

 a black dog book

Published by
Sundance Publishing
33 Boston Post Road West
Suite 440
Marlborough, MA 01752
800-343-8204
www.sundancepub.com

Copyright © text Shane Nagle
Copyright © illustrations Shane Nagle

First published 2001 by
Pearson Education Australia Pty. Limited
95 Coventry Street
South Melbourne 3205 Australia
Exclusive United States Distribution: Sundance Publishing

Guided Reading Level J
Guided reading levels assigned by Sundance Publishing using the text characteristics
described by Fountas & Pinnell in the book *Guided Reading,* published by Heinemann.

ISBN 978-0-7608-4975-0

Printed by Nordica International Ltd.
Manufactured in Guangzhou, China
June, 2014
Nordica Job#: CA21400927
Sundance/Newbridge PO#: 227820

Contents

Characters

Sarah is a computer whiz. She loves to play computer games.

Matt is always laughing.

Jodie is a good friend.

Patrick cares about animals.

Chapter One

Something Weird

On Monday at lunch, Sarah was watching as Matt opened his bag. She saw him make a strange face. So Sarah knew something was wrong with him.

Sarah often noticed things like that.
Sarah liked to watch people closely.

"What's the matter?" asked Sarah.

Matt groaned. "I must have left my sandwich at home. But I found this quarter in my lunch bag."

The next day, the same thing happened to Jodie. "Oh no," she said. "I forgot my sandwich. But why is there a quarter in my lunch bag?"

On Wednesday, Matt's sandwich was gone again. "That's strange," said Matt. "I know I packed my sandwich today, but there's a quarter here instead."

That's when Sarah began to wonder.

By Thursday, Sarah knew she was right. "Hey! This time my sandwich is gone, and I have a quarter, too," she shouted. "This is weird."

Chapter Two
The Plan

Everyone gathered around.

"Something's going on," said Sarah.

"What should we do?" asked Jodie.

"What we need is a plan," said Sarah.

"We could lock our sandwiches in a safe," said Matt.

"Too complicated," said Jodie. "Besides, where could we find a safe?"

Then Sarah noticed Patrick sitting by himself. He wasn't listening to them. He wasn't eating lunch either.

Sarah went over to talk to him. "Is your sandwich missing, too, Patrick?" she said gently.

"No," said Patrick. "Not today." Then he wandered away.

That's when Sarah had an idea.

After school, Sarah set to work. Tap, tap, tap, went her fingers on her keyboard. She was making up a computer game that would help them find the Sandwich Snatcher.

Chapter Three

The Game

At dinner, Sarah ate quickly so she could get back to work. She was still tap, tap, tapping on her computer when her dad told her to turn off the light.

The next morning, Sarah started to work on the computer game again. By the time breakfast was ready, Sarah was ready, too. Game. Map. Plan.

At school, Sarah told her friends she
had made a new computer game. The kids
couldn't wait to try it. When the lunch bell
rang, they gathered in the library.

Sarah stood in front of them, just like a teacher. "OK, everyone," she said. "I hope you like my new computer game. It's called *The Alibi*."

"Sounds exciting," said Matt.

"This game is about some things you did last week. You must answer some questions," said Sarah. "And you have to use the map to mark your locations."

"The computer game tells you what to do. Does anyone have any questions?" asked Sarah. She studied all of the faces looking at her. No one said anything.

"OK," said Sarah. "Let's begin."

Sarah leaned forward and gave a signal. All of the computer screens in the library began to flicker and whir into action.

"Wow!" said Matt.

"Whoa," said Jodie. "This is going to be fun!"

Sarah's friends began to play the game. They looked at their maps very closely.

There was a different map for each day. On each day, the children marked their positions on each map. They also typed in who they played with before school each day of the week. And every kid had to remember where they had left their lunch bags each day. They had to type that in, too.

Sarah kept her eyes on the data. She was busy looking at everyone's answers. She wanted to find out who didn't have an alibi.

And then it happened. Patrick's data did not match up. Sarah realized that he must know what was going on. She knew she had to talk to Patrick.

Everyone was laughing and chattering. Playing *The Alibi* had been a lot of fun.

"Hey, Sarah, that was cool," said Matt.

"Yes," said Jodie. "You're smart, Sarah."

Sarah just stared at her computer. She wished she hadn't found the Sandwich Snatcher.

Then something awful happened.
Patrick looked like he was going to cry.

When the kids noticed Patrick's face, they stopped fooling around. They watched as Sarah put her hand on Patrick's arm.

Jodie looked at Matt. Matt looked at Patrick. For a moment everyone was quiet. Patrick stared down at his keyboard. Matt started to giggle, but all of the other kids glared at him, so he stopped.

Chapter Four
Patrick's Problem

The kids watched as Sarah typed something on Patrick's computer. "What's going on?" she typed.

Patrick took a deep breath. "I'm sorry everyone," he typed. Then Patrick turned bravely to his friends. "Last week I found some puppies—five little puppies and their mother. They were really hungry, and I wanted to help them," he said.

"But I couldn't take them home. My
dad doesn't like dogs. And I was scared.
I thought that if anyone found out, the
puppies would be taken to the dog pound,"
Patrick said.

The kids looked at each other.

"I'm really sorry," said Patrick. "I fed them my sandwich, but it wasn't enough."

No one needed to hear any more.

"What are their names, Patrick?" asked Sarah.

"What color are they?" asked Matt.

"Are they soft and cuddly?" asked Jodie.

The kids had so many questions, Patrick had trouble answering them.

Sarah took Patrick by the hand. "Let's go see the puppies," she said gently. "I've still got some lunch left."

"Yeah!" said Matt. "So do I. Let's go."
The kids headed off, with Patrick leading
the way.

They walked to Patrick's secret location.
It was at the far end of the playground.

Patrick led them to a large bush. Under the bush, they saw the mother dog and her puppies. They were snuggled up in a box that Patrick had brought from home.

The mother dog let Patrick pick up the puppies. The kids squeezed in to get a closer look.

Before the end of lunch, the kids had fallen in love with the puppies. They each agreed to bring extra sandwiches and to help find homes for the puppies.

"My gran might take care of them until we can find homes for them," said Jodie. "But we'd have to help her."

Chapter Five
The Schedule

Now Sarah and her friends are very
busy helping Gran take care of the puppies.

Sarah keeps the schedule on her computer. That way, all of the kids know which puppy needs to be walked, and when.

The schedule also tells the kids whose job it is to help feed the puppies and take them to puppy school.

And once a week, all of the kids go to Sarah's house. They talk about the puppies and play their favorite computer game— *The Alibi*.